HOW TO START A BUSINESS AND BE YOUR OWN CEO

DEBORAH GORMAN

Copyright 2015 Deborah Gorman
Published by Deborah Gorman at Smashwords

All rights reserved.

ISBN: 1511984376
ISBN-13: 978-1511984379

Acknowledgements

Thank you to members of Chapel Hill Leads for graciously taking time to answer a few of my questions about their businesses: Elizabeth Burke, Bruce and Sarah Vance, James Asbill, Maryanne Hubbard, Doug Linn, and Don Emmett. I appreciate your help.

CONTENTS

	Acknowledgements	iii
	Preface	vi
1	Downsized? Start a Business, and Employ Yourself	1
2	Small Is Beautiful: Home-Based Businesses	6
3	Affordable Health Care Act Boosts Entrepreneurship	9
4	How to Plan Your Route to Business Success	13
5	One Hundred Business Ideas	16
6	The Wellness Revolution Still Trending	20
7	Green Businesses	22
8	Food Truck	25
9	Airbnb	30
10	Pet Businesses	33
11	Cleaning & Home Maintenance	35
12	Five Tips for Starting Your Home Business	36
13	Start Your Business Part or Full Time?	38
14	Finding the Why for Your Business	40
15	Ten Steps to Starting a Business	42
16	Franchising	44
17	Network Marketing	49

18	Affiliate or Network Marketing: What's the Difference?	54
19	Multiple Businesses	58
20	The Truth about a Sole Proprietorship	60
21	Business Marketing 101	63
22	Marketing-- Going the Distance	65
23	Networking Online and Offline	67
24	Six Ways to Find More Local Leads	69
25	Avoiding the Debt Trap	71
26	Secrets of Effective Prospecting	74
27	Monitoring Costs and Returns	76
28	Measuring Business Results at Year's End	78
29	Types of Business Structures	80
	Bibliography	83
	About Deborah Gorman	84

Preface

Over the course of my working life, I have started a number of small business ventures. When I was in college I began to feel bored and restless. I'm an entrepreneur at heart. I have a strong spirit of independence and prefer to be my own boss rather than working for others.

My first enterprise was partnering with my husband as a commercial beekeeper and honey producer for several years. We wanted to live simply like pioneers and raise our food organically. We were outliers then, but now the movement towards organic and green businesses has gone main stream.

After that, I have worked as a freelance writer and photo journalist, pastor, a private reading instructor, online book seller, author, and network marketer.

Some have been more successful than others, but I have learned from my failures as well as my successes. Some have been more successful than others, but I have learned from my failures as well as my successes. The book started with some blogs I wrote from my own experiences in business. My purpose in writing is to provide a guidebook to the basics of getting started in business that touches on some current trends in entrepreneurship.

How to Start a Business and Be Your Own CEO is an idea book that explores possible concepts for business start-ups. Drawing on your own unique experience, talents and skills, is the way to find your own business niche that is right for you. Above all, a business should be based on your own interests and passions.

As a handbook, How to Start a Business and Be Your Own CEO provides helpful information about the start-up process, and the basic steps to planning and launching a business.

1 DOWNSIZED? START A BUSINESS AND EMPLOY YOURSELF

"Every beginning comes from some other beginning's end."-- Seneca

In the fallout after the Crash of 2008 and the Recession that followed, millions of people lost their jobs due to downsizing or business closure. Being unemployed long-term, for months and even years became a common situation as there simply were few jobs available, certainly nowhere near enough to meet the demand. For many, months of fruitless searching and sending out resumes became a frustrating, demoralizing ordeal of continued rejection.

Long-term unemployment particularly affected those persons who were 45 years and up in age They remained the lingering casualties of the Great Recession as they doggedly persisted in seeking work, sending out resumes, while trying to keep a positive attitude in the face of repeated rejection.

Some believed that if only they could be granted an interview, they were certain that they would be hired. They experienced a range of emotions, from bewilderment to frustration, anger and depression. There was an amazing amount of passivity expressed as well, as they soldiered on in their belief that just sending out enough resumes must eventually result in an interview and a job offer. But sadly that was not the case.

The struggles of Mike, a draftsman, Elizabeth, a health care writer, and Julie an account manager to cope with their situations were typical.

Mike had used continuing education to upgrade his skills, but still found no job offers, for several reasons, including his age, being passed over for younger applicants with more experience, or as a result of positions being outsourced overseas, and so on. Yet Mike was inflexible, apparently unwilling to try other occupations, in denial and sinking farther into depression.

Elizabeth, on the other hand, had been more flexible and was hired for several positions in addition to freelancing, but she was nevertheless unable to secure a permanent job. Over a number of years Elizabeth continued to cycle in and out of employment. Julie relocated to be closer to family, but had no success in finding a position that matched her qualifications. She was able to get by through a combination of Social Security and a part-time position.

There were no easy solutions. The fact is that this age group was vulnerable for a number of reasons, including the high cost of health care insurance for their age group, as well as the rapid pace of change. Over the course of their working life time, the certainty that one can expect to have one career until retirement has vanished.

Certainly flexibility and a willingness to change and adapt to changing conditions are essential to survival at any age and in any economy. Jim Rohn said, "In order for things to change, you have to change."

There comes a time when one must come to terms with things as they are and accept the reality for what it is and then decide what one can do about it. For starters, making a conscious decision to be in control of your future, rather than waiting for someone else to come along with an offer for you can be the beginning of freedom, and taking back your life.

One solution to being jobless is to create your own employment by starting a business. It's not a simple solution by any means, but it can be a way forward. for those who have the grit and determination to be persistent and work long hours for no pay check in the beginning.

Unemployment benefits for some are more than a safety net, as with careful management, they are a resource which can be used to leverage a business start-up.

Some long-term unemployed individuals started their own business, such as David Walker, a Michigan man who was laid off from a telecom job who told his story on National Public Radio. He qualified for unemployment benefits, which helped to pay his mortgage.

"In 2007, I was laid off with six months severance pay. At the time, jobs were available so during my severance period, I decided to have a go at running a home business. I put our savings into starting this business, which was going to supply garage cabinets and flooring to that growing segment of the housing industry. As we prepared to launch this new venture in late 2007, that industry was turned upside down," David recalled.

He continually sent out resumes in the telecom field, but received no offers. Meanwhile, he started a website for retail sales of closet components. A few orders began to trickle in, slowly at first, just enough to pay for the website expense. Meanwhile he continued to apply for jobs for two more years, but wasn't hired. In the spring of 2010, just as his unemployment benefits were set to expire, the Internet orders increased so that he was earning enough to pay the mortgage and car payments.

David's experience shows that it is possible to start a business with very little money if one is willing to put in long hours and not give up even if there are no profits in the beginning. One problem with many business start-ups is that people expect to receive an instant paycheck. More often than not, however, there is little money coming in at the start, so they give up too soon.

If you find yourself unemployed, you might consider creating a job for yourself by starting your own business. In the short term, it won't be easy. But then, neither is the daily discouragement and rejection that comes with unemployment. In the long run, you just might find yourself better off by taking charge of creating your own future.

Clergy and Non-profit Employees Face Retirement Income Shortfall

Many individuals such as clergy who have spent their career working for non-profit organizations are also finding their retirement savings to be inadequate.

A 2010 article in USA Today, "Many Clergy Ill-Prepared for Retirement," profiled a retired New England pastor who was living on $1200 a month in Social Security and pension, and qualified for food stamps. Pastor Matthews said that he had lost much of his pension funds in the economic crash, then had to keep his thermostat set at 52 degrees during the New Hampshire winter to afford heat. He was selling his home at a loss and moving to Sweden so he could afford health care.

While most clergy are not in such dire straits, many of them have financial problems in retirement. Like persons from other occupations, pastors may fare better or worse in retirement depending on choices they have made and their approach to planning. Some denominations have well-managed retirement plans and offer financial education for the clergy, while others may provide little or no plans at all.

And some pastors have put all their trust God to provide, and did not attend the planning seminars or paid little attention to saving and investing for retirement.

$70,300 was an estimate of the average pay for senior pastors in large congregations. Most clergy, however, serve at lower salary scales. Few small and medium size churches are able to afford that level of compensation. According to a 2008 Southern Baptist compensation study, there were 1,747 churches from all 50 states surveyed that had average attendance between 100 to 500 and annual receipts between $100,000 and $500,000. The average compensation (salary and housing) for a senior pastor in those churches was $51,539. Their average total package, including all benefits was $62,208.

Since most clergy have lived in housing provided by their church as a benefit, they may not own a home once they retire, and housing becomes an added cost in retirement. Also some denominations have quite low base salaries, so the clergy are bi-vocational pastors who work at another full-time or part-time job during the week.

Nevertheless, whether a pastor serves as a full-time or part-time clergy, ministry is not a high-paying vocation in most cases. And it is true that many clergy, along with others who have worked in the service or helping vocations for non-profits, may find it difficult to make ends meet in retirement.

If you are a retired clergy or other non-profit professional who is stretched to make ends meet, you may be searching for resources and information on creating an additional income stream.

2 SMALL IS BEAUTIFUL; HOME-BASED BUSINESSES

"Everyone is an entrepreneur. The only skills you need to be an entrepreneur are the ability to fail, to have ideas, to execute on them, and to be persistent, so even as you learn you move on the next adventure."-- Jim Altucher

What do Amazon, Apple Computer, Hershey's, Mary Kay Cosmetics, and the Ford Motor Company have in common? All of these corporations all were started as home-based businesses. In fact, more than half of all U.S. businesses are based out of an owner's home.

Starting a home-based business has potential advantages and as well as significant challenges.

From a practical standpoint, you can save on initial expenses if you are able to work from home.
First, does your home have adequate space? Can you live and work in the same area? Consider the following questions:

Where in the home will the business be located? What adjustments to living arrangements will be required, and what will be the cost of any necessary changes? How will your family react? Is there enough space away from distractions?

Check on how your local government's zoning ordinances may affect your business. Not knowing the potential legal and community problems and the rules that apply to having a business at home, can have devastating consequences.

Benefits of starting a business in your home
About half of US businesses are home-based, according to the Internal Revenue Service. Launching a business can be a huge challenge, but starting out in your home gives you a number of advantages. You can begin as small as you want and have the convenience of fitting it in to your schedule and lifestyle.

Five advantages of starting your business in your home:
1. Tax advantage:
One important reason for starting your own business is the tax-savings that you can immediately receive on any expenses that you incur for running your business. These include your initial start-up costs as well as other expenses.

There are resources available online from the United States Government Internal Revenue Service regarding what types of expenses are eligible.

The IRS has a helpful site for small business owners. You can find downloadable guides regarding rules and eligible expenses at the Internal Revenue Service: www.irs.gov/businesses/small.

Every North American taxpayer who works a full-time job and does not have a side business could be over-paying taxes by as much as three to nine thousand dollars a year, according to Sandy Botkin, CPA, founder of the Tax Reduction Institute. By using your home as your main place of business, you can claim business-related deductions from your tax return. Consult your tax accountant for the applicable rules.

You may deduct your regular expenses such as office expense for your home office, advertising, accounting and tax preparation, travel and transportation, insurance, phone bills, and more.

2. Significant financial potential is possible. Eliminating high overhead costs such as rent, franchise fees, and hiring employees boosts your profit. As an employee your earnings are limited to what your employer pays you. As a business owner, you earn a profit that can increase as your business expands. Earning profit provides the incentive for growing your business.

3. Less stress is a bonus because you are free to set your own goals, make your own decisions and control your work environment instead of fitting in to meet some one else's demands and expectations. You can save on time and eliminate commuting expenses. Most workers spend hours every work day commuting to and from their jobs. When your office is at home, you can reduce the amount of travel time in your work significantly.

4. Time freedom is a plus as you balance your work and personal life. You can control your own schedule, as long as you are able to keep focused and accomplish your goals. When you control your calendar you are able to do the things you have always wanted to do.

5. Family involvement is a key benefit for many home business owners. You can have a division of labor, as well as support system. Parents can be at home to care for children instead of taking them to day care.

These are just five ways you can benefit by starting your business in your home. There may be other advantages you discover in your own venture.

3 AFFORDABLE CARE ACT BOOSTS US ENTREPRENEURSHIP

"There is much that public policy can do to support American entrepreneurs. Health insurance reform will make it easier for entrepreneurs to take a chance on a new business without putting their family's health at risk."-- Eric Ries

Health insurance is now available to nearly all business owners. Due to the Affordable Care Act in the US, health insurance is no longer linked to a benefit package for full time employees. This is especially beneficial to small start-up business owners who previously would have few options for affordable health insurance.

The Affordable Care Act, which many feared would create challenges for businesses, actually benefits small business, and one particular group of business people: entrepreneurs.

One in four small business owners in the U.S. have been uninsured. The number one benefit of the Affordable Care Act for entrepreneurs and business owners is that they can now afford their own health insurance. In fact, the Affordable Care Act creates eligibility for 83 percent of previously uninsured small business owners. Additionally, many small business owners who currently buy their own individual health care coverage in the private market may now be eligible to take advantage of new cost savings as well.

Joshua S. was reluctant to give up his grocery store job, which had provided excellent health care for him and his family. He had a pre-existing condition that had prevented him from getting insurance in the private market, but being able to get coverage outside of his job helped convince him to quit and start a farm.

"One of the biggest factors was the Affordable Care Act-- that our family would be able to be covered by health care starting the beginning of 2014, he said."

Now, the young entrepreneur is farming on 26-acres in Oregon., where his free-roaming chickens till through the flower beds and goats graze on the lawn. He has 3,000 egg-laying hens, whose eggs he and his partner will sell in the Portland metropolitan area. Soon, they'll add pigs and raise chickens for meat.

It had been hard to leave a job that provided health care, especially since he had trouble getting coverage in the past.

"I was ineligible for any health care. I'd been denied by five different companies because I have back problems," Joshua said, due to having three broken vertebrae in his back. "Nobody wanted to cover me because of that."

So-called job lock, or entrepreneur lock had been holding him in his job..

"Entrepreneur lock has proven to be a significant barrier to potential entrepreneurs," says Dane Stangler, vice president of research and policy at the Kauffman Foundation, which promotes entrepreneurship.

"To the extent the Affordable Care Act unlocks that job lock — that entrepreneur lock — one effect is to provide a boost to entrepreneurship overall," Stangler says.

The U.S. system of employer-provided health care deterred people from quitting a job to start their own business, says Susan Gates, one of the authors of a 2011 Rand Corporation study. "People considering leaving a job with good health insurance faced a daunting challenge in purchasing health insurance on the individual market," Gates says.

The study reported that this particular challenge was reducing the number of entrepreneurs. It also calculated that making health insurance more accessible and affordable in the individual market could increase self-employment and entrepreneurship by a third.

"There's no question that the health exchanges provide a set of opportunities that didn't previously exist," Gates says.

Stangler believes the Affordable Care Act could help boost employment by creating somewhere around 25,000 additional new businesses each year. He's not overly concerned that the employer mandate for companies with 50 or more workers might hurt entrepreneurship as few companies ever get that big, he says.-- John Ydste NPR

At every level, restless employees are celebrating the chance to jump ship. As many as 2.3 million Americans are expected to leave their jobs because of the Affordable Care Act.

Studies indicate that 68 percent of workers value benefits over salary. With health insurance now widely available, employees are no longer shackled to the corporate world. From the front line to the boardroom, closet entrepreneurs are just waiting for the justification to go out on their own. Others see a chance to retire early. Lower paid workers hanging on to jobs for the health care plan see Obamacare as their opportunity to start their own businesses and build wealth.

Not only lower paid workers, but many executives are leaving the corporate world to explore more purpose-driven work as entrepreneurs. They also have noted changes in the business landscape, along with health care costs, as a reason for exiting corporate. For many, the Affordable Care Act is giving talented executives the 'push' they need to leave."

"All things considered, I think the Affordable Care Act is actually a major step towards creating a more prosperous America — because as entrepreneurs and business owners, it enables us to provide a better life for those who help make our success possible everyday."--Richard Lorenzen, Forbes

Atlanta resident Rachel J. loved her job as a director at a global consulting company, but the pace of the job was starting to affect her chronic health condition.

"I needed to work part time and with a flexible schedule. But before Obamacare, I couldn't leave my corporate job without losing my health insurance or paying the exorbitant fees for COBRA," she said.

She was un-insurable by an individual plan due to pre-existing conditions before Obamacare. Both she and her husband had been relying on her full-time job for coverage. "Thanks to the Affordable Care Act," she said, "we don't have to make career decisions anymore based on health insurance." Tasha Eurich, Entrepreneur

4 HOW TO PLAN YOUR ROUTE TO BUSINESS SUCCESS

"If you don't know where you are going, any road will take you there." -- Lewis Carroll, Alice's Adventures in Wonderland.

If you were building a house, you would start from the foundation and build the structure on the foundation. But before you began the foundation, you would need plans, building materials, laborers, and financing. Going into business is a similar process, but sadly many entrepreneurs do not spend enough time laying the groundwork for their enterprise.

Charting your Course
Many businesses just seem to happen. An example is someone who has some money to invest and they decide to buy a business. They find one for sale and decide to buy it even though they lack knowledge or experience with the particular business. Or another person may decide to offer a service without first determining how they will find and get customers. Jack loved to cook. He had gone to school for culinary arts and worked for a large caterer. But he dreamed of having his own restaurant. He found a little cafe in a small town, but there wasn't much parking available. Details like location and parking are critical to the success of a restaurant or retail shop. If customers can't find a parking space nearby, they won't stop.

There are many reasons to start a business. Obviously the greatest reason for starting a business is to make a profit. An additional incentive is that many business expenses including a home office may be tax deductible. Knowing why you want to have a business is a key starting point.

Here are five basic questions to consider:

Why start a business?
What type of business is right for me?
Who will be my customer?
What is my vision?
What resources do I need to begin?

Do you have a talent for creating items that you could sell online, such as handcrafted clothing, jewelry or accessories? Or do you have valuable expertise and skills that you can use to help others?

Next, ask who would want or need your service or product? Is it something that you would make available within a local community, such as home maintenance, catering, or tutoring?

Who is your customer? How will they benefit from what you have to offer?

Are there currently enough other businesses serving these customers, and meeting this need?

Once you have determined your reason for starting a business, and the type of business you wish to start, then you will have answered the basic questions of what you want and why. You should next write a statement that summarizes your vision. Having a vision statement is essential for keeping focused on your dream. You will need to review your vision each day as your proceed.

Next you must consider your resources. How you will finance your project is a critical question. It is best to use your own funds from savings rather than borrowing. The days of easy credit and maxing out credit cards to fund business start-ups contributed to the recent economic crash and recession of 2008. It is possible to start a business on a shoestring if you are creative and resourceful.

You should open a business checking account, and keep all of your business expenses and receipts separate from your household accounts. When starting out, keep in mind how much of your investment you can afford to risk. Say you had $5000 to start, would you be willing to risk losing that entire $5000 if your business does not work out? Additionally, keep in mind that you will undoubtedly need money for operating and other expenses, say for example, marketing and inventory.

What is your plan?
Finally, you should put together a plan for how you will launch your business. You might set initial goals for setting up your website, publicizing, networking and so forth. Decide how much time you will spend.

In the beginning, you will only be able to estimate how much time it takes to accomplish various tasks. A plan at this point is just an outline. It's not set in concrete. It is a reference to help you know what is working. If it's not working, try to figure out why. Inevitably not everything will work as you envision. Then you can go back and revise the plan, and make changes in what you are doing.

Plan, prepare and proceed is a formula for successfully launching any enterprise.

5 ONE HUNDRED BUSINESS IDEAS

"Small opportunities are often the beginning of great enterprises."-- Demosthenes

There are multiple options to starting a business. You can be an entrepreneur, who comes up with your own idea and plan to start a business from scratch. Another route to getting into business is to buy an existing business that is for sale. You can also partner with a franchise or direct selling company.

What kind of business should you start? Do you have a product to sell, or a service to offer? Here are 100 small business ideas:

Accounting/ Bookkeeper
Airbnb
Air Duct Cleaner
Antique Furniture Restoration
App Developer
Appliance Repair Technician
Blogger
Business Broker
Business Consultant
Cabinet/ Furniture making
Candy Maker
Carpenter
Catering Service
Cell phone repair
Composting
Computer Repair and Maintenance
Construction Cleanup
Cupcake Baker

Data Entry Service
Desktop Publishing
Dog Trainer
Doula
Drop Shipping
Editor/Proofreader
Electronic Shopping & Mail Order
Event planner
Food Truck/Food Cart Operator
Florist
Freelancer
Furniture Mover
Gardener
Genealogist
Gift Basket
Grant Writer
Green Cleaner
Green Consultant
Gutter Cleaner
Hair Salon Owner
Handmade Crafter
Handyman
Hauling Services
Home Caterer/ Personal Chef
Home-Based Child Care Provider
Home Care Services
Home Stager
Home Weatherization Professional
House Painter
Ice Cream or Frozen Yogurt Shop Business
Ink and Toner Cartridge Refilling
Interior Designer
Internet Advertising/marketing
Internet Reseller on eBay, Amazon, Etsy
Internet Technology
Jewelry Maker
Landscaper
Laundry Service

Lawn Mowing/Yard Maintenance
Lawn Mower/ Small engine repair
Life Coach
Locksmith
Marketing Copywriter
Massage Therapist
Medical Billing
Medical Transcriptionist
Motivational Speaker
Motorcycle Repair
Nanny
Network Marketer
Nutrition Consultant
Online Copywriter
Organic Lawn Care Provider
Personal Concierge
Personal Trainer
Pest Control Professional
Pet Boarding
Pet Counselor
Pet Groomer
Pet Sitter/ house sitter
Photo Restoration Service
Photographer
Pizza Parlor
Pool Cleaning and Maintenance Provider
Private Tutor
Professional Organizer
Project Manager
Resume Writer
Sandwich Shop
Senior Care Provider
Snow and Ice Removal Service
Solar Energy Installer
Social Media Consultant
Software Publishers
Translation Service Provider
Tour Bus Host

Video Producer
Virtual Assistant
Web Designer
Wedding Planner
Wellness Instructor
Yoga/Pilates Instructor

6 THE WELLNESS REVOLUTION STILL TRENDING

"Wellness industry products and services have perhaps the strongest legs of any product or service, as people immediately notice when someone has a wellness experience and are anxious to duplicate the results." -- Paul Zane Pilzer

Beth Burke started Vital Living Healing Arts, a massage therapy business, in her home. Her reason for starting her own business was typical of many new entrepreneurs. After Beth had lost her job, she wanted independence. She was looking for more meaningful work, not just another job. So she went to school to learn massage therapy and got her license. She enjoys helping her clients to with stress management and other health problems, and rates her current satisfaction as very high.

The trend toward health and wellness continues over ten years on since Paul Zane Pilzer first published The Wellness Revolution. In that book, Pilzer predicted explosive growth in the health and wellness field over the next decade. That growth trend continued through the years of a weak economy. Health and wellness has been one of the strongest and most recession resistant areas of the economy.

There are signs of this all around. Today growing numbers of persons, led by the Baby Boomers, but now closely followed by Gen X, Gen Y and Millennials, are going to alternative health practitioners who emphasize prevention rather than treatment of disease.

A growing awareness of the health effects of the many toxic chemicals which are used in agribusiness as well as concerns about the use of hormones, antibiotics and general inhumane practices of raising livestock has contributed to the rising popularity of organic foods. Organic products, which have been raised without the use of chemical fertilizers, toxic pesticides, hormones and antibiotics, are a strong growth area in agriculture.

Fitness and exercise venues are also areas that continue to expand although impacted somewhat by the recession when some people cut back on their spending for monthly memberships. Yoga, martial arts, jazzercise, health clubs, and other programs remain popular as people realize the value of physical activity for health and well-being.

These health trends are the result of increasing numbers of people who desire to take more control over their personal health and well-being, by seeking more choices both in their diet and their options for physical fitness as well.

7 GREEN BUSINESSES

The huge growth of organic and eco-friendly products on retail store shelves is more than just a passing fad. As consumers seek healthier alternatives, organic farming has morphed from the fringes of agricultural producers to main stream, as organic produce, dairy and other products are now readily available even in chain grocers such as Wal-Mart.

Along with that is the mushrooming number of Farmers Markets where shoppers are able to buy locally produced food items ranging from flower plants and herbs, fruits and vegetables, honey, dairy, meat, poultry, and even baked goods directly from the producers. As more people become health conscious, the market is booming for locally produced organic products.

This growing trend presents opportunities for environmentally minded entrepreneurs who are ready to start their own small business. Successful green businesses not only benefit the environment, but also use green business practices as a means to market their products.

Other types of green businesses include green cleaning, organic landscaping, and installation of sustainable energy systems such as wind, solar and geothermal.

If you are thinking of starting a green business, consider these tips:

Find Your Niche
Because the eco-friendly lifestyle appeals to more consumers, there is an increasing potential for new businesses. Production of food, cosmetics and cleaning supplies are growth areas in the organic sector. To be successful, look for ideas that match your own interests.

Get Certified
To differentiate your product or service as environmentally sound, consider obtaining certification from an independent, third-party. Certification allows you to display an ecolabel on your product's label and other marketing materials. An ecolabel is a label which identifies overall, proven environmental preference of a product or service within a specific product/service category. This ecolabel is important for marketing to green customers, and can enhance the value of your brand, because consumers look for ecolabels when they shop.

Organic certification is a certification process for producers of organic food and other organic agricultural products. In general, any business directly involved in food production can be certified, including seed suppliers, farmers, food processors, retailers and restaurants.

Requirements vary from country to country, and generally involve a set of production standards for growing, storage, processing, packaging and shipping that include:

Avoidance of synthetic chemical inputs (e.g. fertilizer, pesticides, antibiotics, and food additives), genetic modification, irradiation, and the use of sewage sludge;

Use of farmland that has been free from prohibited chemical inputs for a number of years (often, three or more);

For livestock, adhering to specific requirements for feed, housing, and breeding;

Keeping detailed written production and sales records (audit trail);

Maintaining strict physical separation of organic products from non-certified products;

Undergoing periodic on-site inspections.

In some countries, certification is overseen by the government, and commercial use of the term organic is legally restricted. Certified organic producers are also subject to the same agricultural, food safety and other government regulations that apply to non-certified producers.

Certified organic foods are not necessarily pesticide-free; certain non-toxic pesticides are allowed.

8 FOOD TRUCK

In the movie, "The Chef", a chef who loses his restaurant job starts up a food truck in an effort to reclaim his creative promise, while piecing back together his estranged family. The film presents a rather romantic picture of starting a food truck business.

In recent years, consumers have increasingly turned to mobile food trucks for breakfast, lunch, dinner and snacks in between. An industry survey by IBIS World placed the annual revenue from food trucks at nearly $1.2 billion in 2009, with growth rates from 2007-2012 near 8.4% annually. The "Street Vendors in the US: Market Research Report" estimated that there are over 15,500 individuals who serve food to diners in open-air locations. Because of their growing popularity, food trucks can be a viable business opportunity.

Food trucks reflect the growth portion of eating out dollars in the U.S. According to a Gallup poll, consumers who eat out of their homes regularly spend more than $100 on a weekly basis, with an average of around $150 each week. Roughly 10% of those surveyed spent over $300 per week, with another 8% spending less than $50. Younger people, and men in particular, eat out more often, according to Forbes.

Costs Vary
In terms of startup cost, there is a wide range for setting up an outside dining venue. Street kiosks can be opened with just a few thousand dollars. Street kiosks generally cost $3,000 to purchase a food cart, $500 for the food ingredients, and around $1,000 to get the necessary permits and rent a space on the street.

If you are looking for the most economical way to start a food truck business, consider a food cart. An ice cream, taco or hot dog cart may not be the most glamorous option, but it is certainly the most feasible way to start for many persons.

Small is beautiful. If you don't want to invest a lot of money, a food cart costs a fraction of a food truck, with many of the same benefits. And if this is your first venture, it can be a way to get your feet wet and learn the business without taking a huge financial risk.

The cost of setting up an actual food truck can easily run into the tens of thousands of dollars. As with any business venture, the costs can be quite low to get a basic operation off the ground or a great deal higher if all the extras are included. The price range could be anywhere from $50,000 upward to $200,000. The higher end of that range would be considered extreme for anything but a high-end establishment that wanted to also have a food truck presence to cater to its customers. On the lower end, anything priced under the $50,000 range might raise concerns about the reliability of the truck or quality of the food preparation equipment.

A rough estimate for launching a food truck operation off is likely between $70,000 and $80,000. A reasonably-priced food truck, such as a used one with only a few years of use that can be renovated to fit a new food focus, will make up the bulk of the cost at around roughly $60,000. Going new would add considerable expense that might not be worth the risk for a start-up venture. Additional expenses include fuel and maintenance, business permits, kitchen equipment purchases or rental expenses, food supplies, insurance, advertising dollars and any employee expenses.

The growing popularity of food trucks means the costs of getting one going also continue to rise. A price tag that should easily run below six figures is well below that of a traditional brick and mortar restaurant, however, which can run anywhere from $100,000 to $300,000 at the low end. A key advantage of a restaurant is that diners know where to find it. In stark contrast, they must be updated on where a food truck will be each day. A regular location is ideal, but the flexibility to drive to where the customers are could be a key competitive advantage for a food truck operator. The mobility of food trucks allows setting up at various events such as festivals or roundups.

A food truck is a difficult business to get started, but it can be done if you have the grit and determination. You will also need patience and persistence to get started, as the start-up time is estimated to be two months to one year or longer.

Husky Hog Barbeque is a successful food truck business started by 38 yr. old Joe and his wife Lauren. Joe had originally dropped out of high school at 17. He disliked being told what to do and was ready to go out into the world. Over the years he tried various things, including being a comedian and got more education. He graduated from college and got a BFA. He also enrolled in a Culinary Institute and graduated with honors. He was unemployed. He developed such a passion for barbeque, that he began entering barbeque competitions and even went to BBQ school. His experience gave Joe a solid foundation for starting his food truck.

Joe and Lauren looked into a food truck, but found the cost prohibitive. They raised money from savings, cashed in retirement accounts and used credit cards, but were still short. Lauren took a business development course. Then a relative loaned them $30 thousand, and with Lauren as a business partner they got a $10 thousand loan from the Womens Business Development Center.

Joe was resourceful and spent a year putting his own truck together by buying used equipment and retrofitting their truck. By taking more time to plan and work it out, they were able to start the business on a shoestring by being creative. This left more funds for other business expenses.

Husky Hog BBQ is not a get rich quick business that has taken a lot of hard work to build on a solid foundation. Now three years in they have added catering and a small restaurant.

Steps to Launching a Food Truck
Because many places either don't allow food trucks or else only allow a limited number of food truck permits at any given time, you will first need to find out whether they are legal in your area. For example, although Los Angeles and New York City are two of the busiest areas for food truck businesses, both cities have caps on the number of permits allowed.

If your city or town allows them, next you should find out where your truck can be open to serve customers. Depending on local ordinances food trucks may not be allowed to park in certain areas.

Once you have a solid plan for where you'll be able to sell your food, you will need to come up with a name for your truck. You should select a unique, memorable name for your food truck that describes your food or theme.

The most successful trucks have a specialty and keep their menu simple. You will also have to decide whether to offer the same menu every day or rotate with daily specials.

Find Financing for Your Food Truck Business. The good news about a food truck business is that is significantly cheaper than a sit-down restaurant. You may still need to get financing from a bank, government small business loan or private investors. Crowd-funding may be a possible source of finding private investors

Stock Your Food Truck. Even if you're able to find a modestly priced used food truck, you will still need to make sure it suits for your particular needs. For hot food, such as pizza, French fries or other fried foods, you will need an oven and deep fryer. If you plan to sell pre-made sandwiches, then you will need ample cooler space. Outfitting a food truck is similar to designing a commercial restaurant kitchen.

Publicize Your Food Truck Business. Even though a food truck is a rolling advertisement on wheels, that doesn't mean you won't have to do advertising and marketing for your business. Social media outlets like Facebook and Twitter are perfect for building a good customer base. You can tweet in the morning where your food truck is heading, to let followers know where you'll be that day.

Most businesses are not nearly as complicated to start as a food truck. If you are passionate about the food truck business, and have the expertise, go for it.

9 Airbnb

Airbnb is a business that you can start if you have an apartment, room, house, or vacation home that you would rent out on a nightly basis. Airbnb is an online marketplace for vacation rentals that connects users with property to rent with users looking to rent the space. Airbnb runs on a marketplace platform model by connecting hosts and travelers and enabling transactions without owning any rooms itself. Unlike traditional hotels or bed and breakfasts, Airbnb grows not by adding inventory but by adding more hosts and travelers and matching them with each other.

It has been trending as it is popular both for travelers who want to stay in an affordable place, as well as owners who want to earn some extra cash by hosting guests in their places.

You can start an Airbnb if you have some property you own but aren't using all the time, such as a second home, condo or apartment. You may even invest in a property to start Airbnb.

Jon, a young entrepreneur bought an apartment to rent out remotely. After first searching Airbnb listings and real estate listings online, he found an apartment for sale in Las Vegas. He paid $40,000 for a one bedroom apartment with a shared swimming pool and tennis court, then he invested $10,000 to upgrade and furnish it. He spent three weeks installing new hardwood floor and painting, and bought new furniture, tv. and three sets of bed linens and towels.

Jon's rental income for the first year was $19,613, average $1,634 per month. His profit was $1,134 monthly and $13,608 the first year.

Because Jon's apartment is remote, his expenses include paying a local housekeeper. He also invested in a Nest which turns off heating and cooling when the apartment is unoccupied, and a Lockitron device for the door. Jon expects to completely pay off his investment in four years.

How It Works
Users start by registering with Airbnb which is free to start. Users are categorized as either Hosts or Guests A valid email address and valid telephone were initially the only requirements to build a unique user profile on the website, however since April 2013, a scan of a government issued ID is now required.

Host user profiles include details such as user reviews and shared social connections to build a reputation and trust among users of the marketplace. Other elements of the Airbnb profile include user recommendations and a private messaging system.

In addition to providing personal information, hosts display listing details including price, amenities, house rules, photos, and detailed information about their neighborhood. Due to the nature of the business, a merit system is in place to allow guests and hosts to leave references and ratings in order to provide evaluations which are displayed to the public.

Creating a listing using Airbnb. Users fill out an online form with initial details. The listing will not go live until the user is ready to publish it. Prices are set by the host. Hosts can charge different prices for nightly, weekly, and monthly stays as well as seasonal pricing. They can advertise their space in the Titles and Descriptions section, outline house rules or other descriptions regarding the residence and publish up to 24 photographs of their place. Airbnb, on a limited basis, is offering free professional photography in most of the listed areas. Profile is a place where the guests can research more about the hosts. This section is often used for hosts to display who they are as well as their philosophies on hosting.

Guests are required to message the host directly through Airbnb to ask questions regarding the property. The host has 100% control over who books their place. When a potential guest puts in a reservation request, the host has at least 24 hours to accept or decline the request.

After the host accepts a reservation, they can coordinate meeting times and contact information with guests. After the reservation is complete, users are encouraged to leave a review. Reviews help build validity and references both for the guests and the host.

10 PET BUSINESSES

Pet related businesses of all kinds are still trending and growing, as pet owners are willing to purchase various products and services to care for their pets

Mary Anne Hubbard has an established business of over eleven years, offering mobile pet bathing and grooming for both dogs and cats.

Previously she had been working as an accountant, but she said, the "prior business I was involved with sold and I was retired for a few years. I looked for a business that I could operate on a smaller scale, operate out of my house, etc....that I enjoyed. What could be better than talking to people about their pets?"

Her Aussie Pet Mobile has grown to nine employees, and in a typical week she works about 40 hours, but says she Would consider it somewhere in between part and full time...."my hours are sporadic but also, since my office is in my house, I often work in the evenings if the phone rings."

Mary Anne described her greatest challenge in the business as maintenance of equipment/vehicles, because they get quite a workout. She would recommend the business to others, but added that it "depends on how involved they like to be; business is much more successful with owner involvement and interest."

David Schmidt and his wife opened Green Beagle Lodge, which offers dog and cat boarding, daycare, grooming and training. David said the business "met our criteria and it seemed as though this area could really benefit from a business with the quality of offerings we envisioned." Their business has been open just a little over a year, and has 24 employees. Being a new business, their greatest challenge at this point is building name and brand awareness as a new business.

11 CLEANING AND HOME MAINTENANCE SERVICES

Bruce and Sarah Vance are the owners of an established cleaning business where they offer carpet, window and general cleaning services for both residential and commercial customers. Their business is divided about 50/50 between janitorial, and residential clients.

Town and Country Cleaning Services ha been doing business for 24 years, and their business has grown to have 34 employees. They report working long hours in their business, averaging 50-60 hours per week.

Bruce said they fell into business in the nineties. He had been trading stock options and lost $35,000, so he wanted to start over at something else. At first they tried painting, then lawn-mowing and cleaning. But the cleaning was the best fit for them. They made a lot of mistakes and learned a lot. They recommend that anyone looking to go into a cleaning business should approach it like a business and check out the trade associations, because doing so will save them years of trial and error, and give them a real leg up. The Association of Residential Cleaning International is a non-profit group that provides information and training resources. Though it seems a simple, easy business, modern cleaning requires knowledge of the science of cleaning.

12 FIVE TIPS FOR STARTING YOUR HOME BUSINESS

"The beginning is the most important part of the work."-- Plato

Patty had some college. She had driven a lecture tour bus for fifteen years, and also had worked in an office. At 53 she was unemployed with no money. Her husband's job covered their bills, but there was little money to spare. She told her husband she thought she could put a tour together. With some help from a friend in a tour company she was able to get started. Patty also got help from a SCORE workshop to learn about business. SCORE is an organization of experienced and retired business people that provides free workshops and counseling. Patty was able to bootstrap her business by reinvesting her profits from a tour to start the next one.

If you're thinking about starting a business, there are many considerations. Here are a handful of tips to help your planning process:

1. Don't use borrowed money if possible. Instead, use your own money from savings. If you don't have savings, be resourceful. Sell some of your possessions that you don't need or use. Find ways to save money by eliminating unnecessary spending in other areas. Do what you can. Start where you are.

2. Learn everything you can about what you want to do and then some. Use resources such as SCORE the United States government Small Business Administration. Attend classes and workshops, research online, read books, listen to tapes, etc. Develop the habit of learning and you will improve your chances to succeed.

3. Network with others to learn what works for them, as well as what doesn't. If you can, get a mentor. Be a mentor for someone else. Often you can get valuable feedback and ideas even from people in different types of businesses.

4. Budget your time and be consistent. Schedule regular hours when you will work on your business, and keep to your schedule as if you were going to a regular job.

5. Set goals and priorities that are measurable and track your progress. Perhaps this is the most difficult. When you set your goal, make a plan for what actions you must take to reach the goal. At first it will be hard to estimate, but if you don't reach your goals, you can then revise the plan for what you will need to do next.

13 START YOUR BUSINESS PART OR FULL TIME?

We all have the same amount of time, seven days a week, twenty-four hours a day. The question is, what we do with the time that we have.

If you are starting a business, you may be tempted to start working full-time in your business as soon as possible. The new entrepreneur, eager to succeed, might assume that the quickest route to success is to devote full-time to the business as soon as possible. It may seem that it will be necessary to be devoting all of one's available energy and time to the effort in order to achieve success. When it comes to starting a business, however, one may actually make more progress when starting on a part-time basis.

We live in a culture of instant gratification fueled by ever faster technology. Because of that, when it comes to starting a business and becoming an entrepreneur, some persons may have unrealistic expectations regarding the amount of time it will take for their business to become profitable enough to replace a full-time income. They may not realize that most business enterprises take some time to become profitable.

Some times less is more, because in the beginning you are bound to make mistakes. Whenever you are doing something new, you will not be able to make the most efficient use of your time and resources. Your lack of experience will inevitably result in your making mistakes along the way.

Even if you think you have spent enough time researching and learning about your new venture, experience is the best teacher.

If you are working full-time at your business, and money is not coming in as quickly as you had expected, it will be more discouraging than if you are only devoting part-time to the effort while still working at a job to provide your income. Working part-time allows you to develop self-discipline and forces you to become better at time management. Before you jump in all the way, you may just want to get your feet wet, and see how you like having your own business.

Even if you are unemployed, it is still better to start your business on a part-time basis. There are various things that you can do to earn money to pay your bills-- even selling online through eBay or Amazon, selling your possessions, or taking temp or part-time jobs. Besides your living expenses, you will also need money for your business expenses as well. So it is preferable if you are able to reinvest your business income instead of drawing on it to pay your living expenses.

Then as your part-time business revenues increase, you will be more encouraged by the amount of income you have been making, since you are only working part-time. You have to remember that your labor is valuable and your goal is to be able to create a profit.

14 FINDING THE WHY FOR YOUR BUSINESS

"Being busy does not always mean real work. The object of all work is production or accomplishment and to either of these ends there must be forethought, system, planning, intelligence, and honest purpose, as well as perspiration. Seeming to do is not doing." -- Thomas A. Edison

Every successful venture begins by answering some basic questions-- what, why how and when? The answers must be a part of laying a solid foundation upon which to build and implement your business plan.

Yet often a would-be entrepreneur rushes into a start-up without completing this crucial planning step. They are aiming to make widgets and sell them to buyers of widgets. Perhaps they know this much, so their planning next moves on to how to make the widgets and get them to the widget buyers. But having neglected to define their purpose, the question of why was not addressed if it ever was considered, and gets lost in the process.

Some years ago I was surprised to hear a youthful entrepreneur remark that he needed to persuade enough clients to subscribe to his services, so that would be able to quit his boring job. His assumption seemed to be that having his own business would not be boring, and that he was in some way entitled to succeed as a means of fulfilling his need to have an exciting career.

His attitude is typical of some would be entrepreneurs who have unrealistic expectations and rush into starting an enterprise without having considered the most basic questions in regard to their purpose. Wishing to escape boring tasks is not a sufficient motivation for becoming an entrepreneur, because any successful venture requires the ability to stick to mundane, boring tasks as well as solving problems on a daily basis.

Having a clear sense of purpose and solid reason why you are doing what you are doing helps to navigate successfully through the obstacles and rough patches you will encounter along the way. A simple answer to why might be to make lots of money for the owner, yet being aware of the reasons for wanting the money gets to the heart of the question of why to answer the motivation question.

15 TEN STEPS TO STARTING A BUSINESS

Starting a business involves planning, making key financial decisions and in some cases completing a series of legal activities. These ten steps can help you plan, prepare and manage your business. Not all of the steps will be applicable to every business. For example if you are a sole proprietor, you may not need to plan for employees at the outset.

Step 1: Write a Business Plan
Your business plan is an outline that will help you map out how you will start and run your business successfully. Your basic business plan should define the what, why, where, when and how of your venture.

Step 2: Get Business Assistance and Training
Take advantage of free training and counseling services such as SCORE (score.org). SCORE is an organization of business mentors who volunteer their time to assist entrepreneurs. SCORE can help with everything from preparing a business plan and securing financing, to expanding or relocating a business.

Step 3: Choose a Business Location
Where will you locate your business? Will you be starting a business in your home, or will you need to have some type of commercial office or retail space? Get advice on how to select a customer-friendly location and comply with zoning laws.

Step 4: Finance Your Business
How much money will you need to finance your business? Depending upon your initial start-up costs, you can use savings, or get financing through government backed loans, venture capital and research grants to help you get started.

Step 5: Determine the Legal Structure of Your Business
Decide which form of ownership is most suitable for your business: sole proprietorship, partnership, Limited Liability Company (LLC), corporation, S corporation, nonprofit or cooperative. You can check the legal requirements in your state.

Step 6: Register a Business Name ("Doing Business As")
Depending on what type of business you plan to start, you may need to register your business name with your local government. You may also want to open a business checking account under your business name.

Step 7: Get a Tax Identification Number
Find out if you will need to obtain a tax identification number from the IRS and your state revenue agency. You may not need one if you don't have any employees, or plan to file Schedule C.

Step 8: Register for State and Local Taxes
Again, depending upon the type of business you start, you may need to register with your state to obtain a tax identification number, or pay sales taxes, workers' compensation, unemployment and disability insurance.

Step 9: Obtain Business Licenses and Permits
Get a list of any federal, state and local licenses and permits that may be required for your business.

Step 10: Understand Employer Responsibilities
If you will be hiring any employees, learn what legal steps will be required.

16 FRANCHISING

"The insurance of working with a big, already successful franchise just gives you the chance to do other things on a more personal level."-- Jason Statham

James Asbill started Ductz, an air duct cleaning business seven years ago after he was downsized from a technical job in North Carolina. "Nobody was hiring people with my skill set," he said. "I looked around for almost a year. I went to a franchise expo and saw this business. My father worked in the HVAC business for many years, so I said I can do this."

James works full time in his business, putting in about 35 hours in a typical week with three employees. He also does carpet cleaning and cleans dryer vents. Overall he has a high level of satisfaction with the business, and says his franchisor delivered on everything they had promised him. James found this business a good fit for his skills and experience, and says that he would recommend the business to anyone with a technical background.

Eight million people are employed in franchises in one out of twelve businesses, according to the International Franchise Association.

Franchising can be attractive if you desire to be your own boss, but the idea of starting from scratch doesn't appeal to you. Franchising offers some guidance and structure in the start-up phase of the business.

A franchise is a business model that involves one business owner licensing trademarks and methods to an independent entrepreneur. Franchises are also referred to as chains.

The two primary forms of franchising are: product/trade name franchising, in which the franchisor owns the right to the name or trademark and sells that right to a franchisee, and business format franchising.

In business format franchising, the franchisor and franchisee have an ongoing relationship, and the franchisor often provides a full range of services, including site selection, training, product supply, marketing plans and even assistance in obtaining financing.

David Schmidt started Zippy Shell, a mobile storage and moving franchise that he started three years ago. He chose the business because he says, "It met our criteria for franchise selection; simple, demand exists, significant differentiator, ability to shape direction, and not too many staff." He works full time and has four employees. He reports being mostly satisfied with it, and feels the franchisor has met most of most of his expectations. His greatest challenge has been with launching a new brand, as the franchisor has only been in the US for 4 years, but he added he would recommend it to others.

Doug Linn started Window Genie, a window cleaning service master franchise, as a second business three years ago. He works full time between two businesses, and has no employees. Overall, Doug is satisfied with both of his businesses. He notes the franchise part has "been slower to develop than I hoped, but it is going okay and I'm happy with it." His greatest business challenge is getting quality leads.

Buying a Work-at-Home Franchise
While home based franchises are becoming more common, but buyers should be aware and watch for potential problems.

Some work at home franchise opportunities are schemes to get your money, so be sure to exercise your due diligence when looking at any opportunity.

Whether it's a restaurant, hotel, auto service shop or retail store, franchising is not without its financial risks. Research conducted for the U.S. Small Business Administration found that only 62 percent of small franchise firms started in 1986 and 1987 were still around by 1991, while non-franchise firms or independent businesses had a 68 percent survival rate. Another study by the U.S. Small Business Administration in 2002 found franchises accounted for over one-third of all retail sales. But it also noted that, as in the earlier study, the failure rate of franchisees was greater than that of independent businesses.

Research the Franchise Before You Invest
Because franchising is a complex and possibly risky decision, you should carefully research the opportunity, to make sure it is the right fit for you.

Before you decide to buy into a franchise business, you need to do a lot of research, because you could stand to lose a significant amount of money if you do not investigate the business carefully before you invest. Franchise sellers are legally required to disclose certain information about their business to potential buyers. Make sure that you get all the information you need first before entering into a franchise agreement.

You should know the answers to the following questions:

How much money can you afford to invest?
What are your abilities and personality style, and is the franchise a match?
What are your goals?

Franchising Strategy
Before investing in a franchise, you should have a strategy. Doing your homework about the franchise first will help you gain a solid understanding of what to expect as well as the potential risks that you will be taking on.

In addition to the routine investigation that should be conducted prior to any business investment, you should contact other franchisees and ask them about their experience with the business. You can obtain a Uniform Franchise Offering Circular (UFOC), which contains vital details about the franchise's legal, financial, and personnel history, before you sign a contract.

Understand What You're Getting Into
Before entering into any contract as a franchisee, you should be completely sure that you would have the right to use the franchise name and trademark, receive training and management assistance from the franchisor, have assistance from the franchisor in marketing, advertising, facility design, layouts, displays and fixtures and have a business territory that is protected from competing franchisees of the same company.

Be Aware of Possible Pitfalls
The contract between the two parties most often benefits the franchisor far more than the franchisee. The franchisee is generally subject to meeting sales quotas and is required to purchase equipment, supplies and inventory exclusively from the franchisor.

Because the tax rules surrounding franchises are often complex, you should have an attorney, preferably a specialist in franchise law, to assist in your evaluation of the franchise package and tax considerations. An accountant may also be needed to determine the full costs of purchasing and operating the business as well as to assess the potential profit to the franchisee.

Pros and Cons of Franchising
Pros:
Franchising is a turnkey system. Support and training are provided by the franchisor, offering the franchisee the opportunity to network with other owners. Other benefits of the system are brand name, lower inventory prices, and easier staffing. It can work well for someone with a managerial background and corporate experience.

Cons:
Franchising has high start-up costs. There are usually additional charges for marketing, as well as on-going royalty costs. Because franchising is a cookie-cutter system, it offers less freedom for innovation. Broken promises can be a problem with some franchises, if the franchisors fail to live up to their promises.

It is essential to do your due diligence and thoroughly research any franchising opportunity before making an investment and committing to a contract. Contact other franchise owners and ask them about their experience. Have your own attorney review the contract with you so that you can make an informed decision regarding both the franchisor's and your obligations and potential liabilities you may incur.

17 NETWORK MARKETING

"The early pioneers of both wellness and network marketing were motivated by the sense that it was possible to create a better life than the conventional routes offered-- better personal health and better economic health, respectively. Now the "alternatives' of yesterday have become the economic powerhouses of today and tomorrow."-- Paul Zane Pilzer

Network marketing is another type of business model, in which a company provides products and distribution to be marketed by independent entrepreneurs. Network marketing is a form of direct selling, where products or services are sold directly to consumers outside of a traditional retail venue, such as a brick and mortar store. The marketer receives a commission on sales orders that are filled directly by the company. The marketer does not have to purchase, store and distribute inventory.

Paul Zane Pilzer said that the direct selling industry may provide one solution to the shrinking job market currently plaguing the economy. Pilzer is an economist and author of nine best selling books, including The Coming Wellness Revolution. He said that the United States is facing a challenge to replace lost jobs with earning opportunities as well as much needed training in new skills.

Modern forms of direct selling include party plan sales, one on one, and or internet sales.

Direct selling encompasses a variety of distribution methods; multilevel marketing is one type of distribution and compensation method. The other type of direct selling would be single level agents, such as insurance agents who do not earn commissions on group sales

In a multilevel distribution model, products are distributed from one level of distributor to another and compensation is based not only on one's own product sales, but also on the product sales volume of one's team. Several states, including Georgia, Idaho, Louisiana, Massachusetts, Montana, Nebraska, Oklahoma, South Dakota, Texas, Washington and Wyoming, statutorily define multilevel distribution companies.

Information dissemination is a key component of direct selling, according to Pilzer. "We have a huge backlog of better products and services that people aren't buying because they don't know about them. Direct selling is the most efficient method for the distribution of intellectual information that will improve your life. It is the ideal model that allows anyone to reach out," he said.

An estimated 15.6 million people are involved in direct selling in the United States and more than 92 million worldwide. Most are women, and nearly a third are men or two-person teams such as couples. The vast majority of network marketers are independent business people – they are micro-entrepreneurs whose purpose is to sell the product and/or services of the company they voluntarily choose to represent – not employees of the company. Legitimate network marketing companies charge a relatively small fee for their starter kits, sell products that are purchased by the ultimate user and normally offer reps refunds for unsold items.

Network marketing companies or MLMs (multi-level marketing) are sometimes erroneously referred to as "ponzi" or "pyramid schemes" – companies structured with the intent of defrauding the public.

Pyramid schemes are illegal, however, because the vast majority of their participants lose money. These scams rely on recruiting new representatives to profit rather than product sales, overcharge reps large upfront fees and convince them to buy large amounts of inventory that is not returnable. Their products generally have little or no actual value, or they may have no products. There are new types of pyramid schemes which purport to pay money for activities such as social media or reading online articles.

The median annual income for direct sales consultants in 2011 was $2,400, according to Amy Robinson, spokesperson for the Direct Selling Association.

While that figure sounds low, approximately 90 percent of all direct sellers operate their businesses part-time, and most work under 10 hours a week.

Also, many reps go into direct sales because they want to buy their favorite products at a discount and have fun earning a little extra spending money. The average earnings figure is lower because reps often get into the business just to buy products for themselves and have no intention of selling or recruiting, Robinson said.

According to Direct Selling Association studies, more than half of direct sellers reported positive net income from direct selling after taxes and expenses. Nearly half of new direct sellers reported a positive net income, by those representing their current company for less than a year, and by nearly half of direct sellers who say that they are not very likely or not at all likely to continue in direct selling in the future. The survey group also includes those sellers who are discount buyers and do not sell products and services to others, thus not generating an income.

In three years Ronald achieved success in USANA, a nutritional supplement company.

Ronald grew up in a single parent family where his mother was in a constant financial struggle. From the age of 12 he was taking responsibility to help bring in more money, hustling with a paper route among other things. As an African American it was hard for him to find jobs. Years later an old friend from college invited him to a business presentation. "I was so intrigued by the possibility to become my own boss and to set my own rules and schedule," he recalls. But things did not change instantly. "I did start something new and wonderful, but it took an enormous amount of work to get going." But Ronald was determined, and he kept going. "I have hope for my future now. Before, I didn't see myself living past 18. I couldn't imagine myself leaving the world I was confined to," but his USANA business changed all that.

Direct sellers report a positive experience with direct selling in other ways as well:

Four in five (82%) direct sellers have been with their current direct selling company for one year or more, and 34% for five years or more.

88% of direct sellers rate their personal experience in direct selling as excellent, very good, or good.

85% of direct sellers say that direct selling meets or exceeds their expectations as a good way to supplement their income or as a way to make a little extra money for themselves.

91% of direct sellers say that direct selling meets or exceeds their expectations as a business where the harder they work the more money they can make.

"The number of hours you invest in your business will determine how quickly you grow," said Mary Christensen, author of Be A Direct Selling Superstar. "Every aspiring direct seller should ask this question: 'Am I prepared to put the time and effort into achieving my goal?' It's not enough to want it. You have to be willing to work for it."

An advantage of the direct selling business model is a low start up cost, which allows people to create new income opportunities for themselves who could not afford to invest in other types of businesses.

With the proliferation of home computers, as well as mobile phones, apps and social networks, the tools are available for millions of people to create new work solutions for themselves working out of their homes.

Some advantages of direct selling include:

An opportunity to create your own opportunity.
Begin where you are, earn while you learn.
Set your own schedule-- work when and where you choose.
Low start-up costs create a level playing field, making it possible for anyone to get started.
Network marketing provides a less expensive alternative to starting a franchise business.
No formal re-training in a technical school, community college or university is required.

18 AFFILIATE OR NETWORK MARKETING: WHAT'S THE DIFFERENCE?

Affiliate marketing is a business that is based on the Internet, through which products are marketed by affiliates who then receive commissions on the sale of the products sold through their sites or ads. The products may be sold either through squeeze pages, link ads or banner ads.

Because affiliate marketing has been promoted so heavily as being an easy way to make money, thousands of people are trying it.

With affiliate marketing you need to research each product to know what you are promoting. How do you tell if the software you are selling actually does what it is supposed to do, or if the weight loss products are even safe?

One problem with affiliate marketing is when dissatisfied customers get a charge-back refund on their credit card, and the commission is then deducted out of the affiliate's account.

While affiliate marketing is touted as an easy system that anyone can do, in fact to succeed at affiliate marketing requires the ability to generate massive amounts of traffic, numbering in the thousands of views before enough people actually click on an ad, and then follow through with a purchase of the product.

There are two common ways to monetize a blog. Affiliate marketing and paid advertising. Either method requires huge numbers of followers.

There are some gurus like John Chow, Shoebox Money, or Matt Bacak who have made great fortunes by affiliate marketing, but they have massive followings, which generate the required traffic. For most people in affiliate marketing, it's a grind and a struggle every day to drive traffic to their ads or pages, and few are making really big money.

Marketers are encouraged to "leverage" their offers by buying pay per click ads on Google or other networks. But effective ppc ads are not easy to write, and require knowing how to select the best key words. Many find that after they pay huge amounts to Google for pay per click ads, their profits are slim.

In addition, Google frequently changes their algorithms, making the process of keywords extremely difficult for those without the technical expertise to create effective advertising. Thus pay per click advertising can be difficult unless one can afford to hire a professional marketer to take care of the ads, which can be extremely costly.

Network marketing is a more social business. Instead of working solo online, network marketers join a team, and get their own customers who provide them with repeat sales and thus the opportunity to earn residual income as they are selling consumable products or services. As the business grows, it offers opportunities for meeting new people, making friends and travel.

Instead of searching for products to sell and researching the products, the products are supplied through the company and the marketers enroll customers and take their orders. The marketer can focus all of their attention on learning one product line, promoting one product line, and business model to their team.

With network marketing you can share your products with anyone you personally know, or also advertise to people you do not yet know, whether online or offline. Thus network marketing is flexible and offers unlimited possibilities to grow your business.

Is Affiliate Marketing a Viable Money-Maker?
Some bloggers have discovered they made little money with their blogs from affiliate marketing commissions while other affiliate marketers claim to have never been able to make money at affiliate marketing. Some say they have tried numerous affiliate opportunities, yet never made any money.

Some estimate that as many as 98% of affiliate markets fail to make any substantial income from their efforts, and that affiliate marketing has passed its prime and so is no longer a viable business model.

Affiliate marketing, unlike network or mlm marketing, is largely an individual home-based venture. By and large affiliate marketers are in business for themselves and may be promoting a range of products through ads or links on their blog or website. John Chow and Matt Bacak are two affiliate marketers who have achieved massive success, because they have huge lists.

Network marketers on the other hand join one company and work as a team with others to make sales.

Both have their own pros and cons. It is largely an individual choice based on one's own preferences.

Another factor in affiliate marketing is that it requires a massive amount of traffic, technical ability in seo, and the constantly changing search engine algorithms.

With a network marketing opportunity you can thoroughly research one company, become an expert and get behind products that you personally use and recommend.

Neither affiliate marketing nor network marketing/direct selling are easy businesses to build. Either one requires massive amounts of effort. Therefore it is best to choose one or the other depending on your personal preference.

As with everything in a business your success in affiliate marketing depends most on the effort that you put into it.

19 MULTIPE BUSINESSES

Everyone should have multiple streams of income. In these uncertain times, the old success formula of getting an education, then getting into a lifetime career with one company is no longer works. Having a stable career with a good middle class income is going away.

The concept of multiple streams of income is ancient. People have always worked at more than one trade or business to make a living, from the time of the nomadic shepherds who bought goods and animals and traded them along their routes.

Multiple small business ventures can be either online or off.

Because many small business ventures fail, creating additional sources of income increases your odds of success. If you establish 3 - 5 or even more highly-niched micro-businesses, not only are you creating additional income sources, but you will also give yourself a better chance of making at least one of your businesses a long-term success.

Another reason to have multiple sources of income is business is cyclical. When you have multiple business projects, you can be working at something on the side during slack times for main business.

Don Emmett owns Entrust Associates, a business brokerage firm for main street, ecommerce businesses. He finds and qualifies buyers for existing, operating business and evaluates the business. Unlike real estate, business is living, breathing thing. Don has run the brokerage for eight years. Prior to that he sold a business in New York. A friend who was a financial planner asked him to help with a client who was selling his business. He then attended a business brokerage conference and decided it would be an interesting business to get into.

Don says his greatest challenge in the business is finding new, quality opportunities to keep in his pipeline. Good businesses sell themselves for the most part, he says. The supply of buyers far exceeds the listings of businesses for sale. He needs to be marketing and networking constantly. His best sources for client referrals are attorneys and accountants.

Besides the brokerage, Don also started a pool and hot tub maintenance business a couple of years ago. He described Aqua Squad as a pool geek in a truck is a with two employees. Don works from home, and in a typical week he works about 45 hours between his two businesses, with the brokerage as full-time and Aqua Squad part time. He enjoys business and rated his level of business satisfaction as very high.

Doug Linn is a business consultant who does leadership coaching and mentoring, and he has also started a window cleaning business through a franchise.

David Schmidt started his mobile storage and moving business first, and then three years later he and his wife opened Green Beagle Lodge, a pet care and boarding business.

20 THE TRUTH ABOUT A SOLE PROPRIETORSHIP

Going to work for myself in a home business had a strong attraction for me, as it does for many individuals, for several reasons. Perhaps the strongest appeal is being on your own, being your own boss.

The business I started was a learning center, with a focus on helping struggling readers. I had heard of a course on phonics that one could purchase which included training. It was not a franchise, and the initial start-up investment included training, learning materials and a license to reproduce them for my own use. I registered my business with the state as a sole proprietorship.

It was exciting and fulfilling. I enjoyed teaching, and because I loved reading, I had always wanted to teach a non-reader how to read. The course was effective, and my students made good progress, even a girl whose parents had been told that she would never learn to read. This gave me true joy.

These successes kept me going through the struggling times of reaching out to get more students. Marketing and promotion were continual challenges, and I neither did them well, nor enough. In the beginning of any business you have to constantly market, and promote, your business.

Eventually I focused more attention on marketing, but it wasn't enough.

There were other problems-- students whose parents could not pay, so they attended sporadically or dropped out. When they didn't show I didn't get paid, even though I had hours scheduled.

The down side of any service business is you are only paid if you are working. In that it is much like a job, only a job in which you don't punch out. You have all the responsibility for everything that happens, what works and doesn't, and you have all the expenses as well.

So when you don't have clients no money is coming in, yet all of your expenses continue. In my case that included ads that I had bought to promote my business for which I had signed contracts. Another drawback to the sole proprietorship for some is the solo part. If you are a person who is extremely independent, wanting to be in control and do everything yourself, it's a good fit.

What I have learned is the value of having a partner in the business, and/or mentor, someone that I could turn to for help and advice. When I had started this business I went to a consultant who helped me draw up a business plan. The plan was for how the business would grow through referrals, and then I would train other teachers to help me teaching more students. The problem was I didn't know how to implement the plan I had drawn up.

There is value in collaboration with others. You can share experiences, get ideas and support. This stimulates creativity and makes for synergy.

My Nanny Gig
After a move to be closer to family, I spent a couple of years caring for my grandson while I settled in to my new environment. I was doing it temporarily while I figured out what I wanted to do-- start back into the business I had been doing, or start something else.

For the most part being a nanny is a pleasant job for anyone who is patient and enjoys young children. I got my cardio workout walking all over town pushing my grandson in the jogging stroller.

When he napped I had some time to work on my own projects, either writing or studying various subjects pertaining to business. I chose to be a nanny while I was making a transition, and because it was for my grandson. That summer I realized that it was a priceless experience that was.

Like other forms of self-employment, if you aren't working your income stops. Being a nanny is an occupation with little opportunity for advancement. While it can be fun and gratifying, it is a form of trading hours for dollars that has limited income potential.

21 BUSINESS MARKETING 101

"The aim of marketing is to know and understand the customer so well the product or service fits him and sells itself." -- Peter Drucker

mar•ket•ing -- märkədiNG/
noun
1. the action or business of promoting and selling products or services, including market research and advertising.

If you own a business or are thinking about starting one, an effective marketing strategy is essential to connect with customers or clients. You can make the most scrumptious pecan pies or be the most incredible violin instructor ever, but if you don't have any customers, you will not stay in business for long. It is crucial to make marketing a top priority.

You should devote 20% of your efforts to marketing, but really in the beginning it would be much more than that, even 100%, because in the beginning, your top priority must be connecting with people and getting leads.

But what is marketing, really? When we think of marketing, what comes to mind is advertising because we are being constantly bombarded with various ads in the media.

In my experience I found marketing to be my greatest challenge, and most business owners agree it ranks either number one or close to the top.

How can you get visibility for your business, and communicate your unique brand. How do you attract clients and customers?

The training course I took prior to launching my learning center business supplied me with some brochures, fliers, business cards and suggestions for community networking that proved to be mostly ineffective. I had some results from ads placed in local newspapers and the yellow pages, but these were costly.

You want to start out by spreading the word to your warm market network of friends, family, neighbors and colleagues where you work or have worked in the past. Not everyone will be interested, but they may help you with word of mouth referrals.

The biggest mistake in marketing is not doing enough. Most people make a few contacts, and if they get no response, they stop. But it will take repeated contacts -- from 4 to 7 to elicit a response. And you also need a large list because only a very small percentage will be interested in what you are offering.

Advertising through traditional channels such as newspapers, radio, TV or joining the Chamber of Commerce is expensive. If you are a small business owner and you're on a limited budget, you must find ways to get exposure at little or no cost.

At the least, your business needs to be online.

The Internet offers several basic services to get visibility. You can start by getting a free Internet listing in Google Places, Bing, Yahoo Local, or other sites such as LinkedIn.

22 MARKETING-- GOING THE DISTANCE

"Marketing is a contest for people's attention." -- Seth Godin

On marketing in tough times, Richard Branson observed, "You just have to do it."

Many small business owners would agree that marketing is their greatest challenge.

With marketing, the huge mistake most people make is not being consistent. They might buy a few ads, but then if they don't get immediate response, they think it didn't work and quit. You may not see instant results. It is always good to test what you're doing, and compare the results to learn what works for you.

Marketing is like an exercise program; doing it once in a while doesn't bring the same results as if you keep doing it every week, or even better every day.

Marketing is more like a marathon than a sprint. It is a long distance from the start to the finish line, but you have to keep going with a lot of boring, repetitive, mundane tasks. Even if you don't have a huge advertising budget, you can send out some post cards and letters to people on your list.

When I started my business I had no money for a marketing budget, because I had spent all of my savings to start up. I decided to start on a shoestring and pay as I went. So, I had my previous business on Amazon, and when I made money on Amazon sales, that was my marketing budget to spend on my promotion.

Send thank you notes to your customers. Sending out a few letters each week can do wonders for your business. Send out press releases monthly.

Social media sites such as Twitter, Facebook, LinkedIn, Google+ and Pinterest are good for increasing your online exposure. Start a blog. You can start a free blog on sites such as Blogger or Wordpress.com as a way to learn about blogging and get a feel for it. If you like video, you start a Youtube channel for your business.

You just have to keep going, and do some marketing every day.

23 NETWORKING ONLINE AND OFFLINE

There is no doubt that the Internet has revolutionized communication, marketing, and networking, so using the Internet should definitely be a part of any serious marketing strategy. It can increase your visibility while helping you to gain recognition as it allows people to gain familiarity with you and what you're about.

An advantage of promoting your business online is that you can reach beyond your locality. You are no longer limited by geography as you can reach out across the globe. This provides greater opportunity if you're living in a small town or rural area and you're in a place where few people are interested in your product. There are many free and low cost options for online business presence, including blogs, social media, search engine listings, websites and advertising.

That being said, however you should not overlook offline marketing entirely either. Many people go online as I did when they find they have exhausted their warm market possibilities.

When I started a network marketing business shortly after moving to a different part of the country, I had very few local acquaintances outside of my immediate family. Besides that, at the time I was working at home as a nanny, so I had few opportunities to go to events where I could meet new people.

At first, I tried to market my business almost entirely online, and I did achieve some success in attracting prospects and customers. But I also found that many people were merely surfing around to different sites looking at information. It often proved difficult to connect with them as they were unresponsive to follow up attempts. Some had even entered fake email addresses and phone numbers to gain access to my site.

While Internet marketing is useful and perhaps even essential in the digital age, one should not rely on it as the sole strategy for building your business. After I got more settled in my location, I began to put more effort into local marketing offline.

I discovered local business networking meetings in my area that were sponsored by the Chamber of Commerce. Networking groups are sponsored by various groups and offer a variety of formats. Checking with the local Chamber of Commerce is a good place to start in finding a group in your area. Usually the format is a meeting at a restaurant or other venue that may include either a meal or light refreshments.

Business Networking International is another organization with many local chapters. My experience with business networking groups has been positive. The members are friendly and helpful. The best way to get a feel for them is by attending a variety of the meetings. You can then decide for yourself how much time you wish to spend with this type of networking

The best way to promote your business is to build relationships with people and help them with their needs, because people do business with people they know, like and trust.

24 SIX WAYS TO FIND MORE LOCAL LEADS

Do you struggle to find enough local leads, because you have few acquaintances due to being a newcomer in the community? Or perhaps you have burned through your warm market already and your friends and family will not listen to yet another opportunity?

Here are six ways that you can do that.

First, you should have a local Internet listing for your business in online directories, starting with Google+ places, Yahoo Local and Bing.

Next, find people with common social interests such as sports, dancing or bowling. It is best to get involved with groups where you will see people more than once. You may want go to a gym or fitness center to get in shape.

You might want to take a class.

Look on meetup.com to find social events and activities with like-minded people.

Volunteer for a charity or community group. There are many worthwhile groups that are always in need of people to help.

Contact the local Chamber of Commerce to find local business networking meetings. There you will meet other entrepreneurs and small business owners who are familiar with the local community. They are looking for referrals and also willing to give referrals as well.

Remember that people do business with people they know, like and trust. Whatever ways you meet new people, it takes time to make the connection and get acquainted. Of course you do not to rush in and start pitching your business. People love talking about themselves. It is good show an interest in them and ask questions to find out what problems they have, and how you may be of help to them. When you show an interest in others and are helpful to them, then they will be interested in what you are doing.

25 AVOIDING THE DEBT TRAP

If you're starting a business, finding money to pay your expenses and build your business is a necessity. Financing with credit cards might seem to be a solution, but it can quickly turn into a trap. During a time of easy credit, it was fashionable for people to "max out" their credit card to finance a business start-up. Using their home as a piggy bank and taking out home equity loans was another way that many people lost their homes when the economy went south.

Using credit cards is a way of life for many people. It's tempting when you suddenly have new expenses to use credit to pay for them, thinking that you will pay them off right away as soon as your cash flow increases. But using credit can be a crutch where you get in to the habit of using it. I learned this the hard way. In a typical business, the income is not consistent and will vary from month to month and some seasons will be slower for the business.

With the high interest rates, monthly credit card bills soon become a burden if your cash flow doesn't grow as fast as you think it will. Getting too deeply in debt is a trap that can sink any business, so it is best to avoid it by any means that you can.

An advantage of pay as you go, or bootstrapping for your business start-up is that since you have to pay cash, it's much easier to define on your priorities. Your priorities are determined by what you can afford, which encourages you to be resourceful, and focus on what is most essential.

When you avoid incurring business debt on which you have to pay interest your expenses are more manageable. You will have less stress without having to carry the weight of a load of debt.

Using Pay as You Go to Start a Lecture Tour Business:
Patty was able to start a successful lecture tour company on a pay as you go basis. She had experience working in the business, and thought she might be able to start her own tour. With help from a friend in a tour company, she put together her first tour and it sold out. She then rented a bus, thus avoiding up front costs. Her clientele were mostly retirees who gave her positive reviews of their enjoyable experience, which spread by word of mouth.

Patty borrowed no money to start her business. After Patty paid for the bus and lunch for her guests, she made a small profit. The money she made off a tour would go into funding the next one. The first year she grossed $12 thousand, and netted $1,500. In the second year, her business grew to a $92 thousand gross and $11,500 net.

In her third year, after Patty hired a financial manager she grossed $92,000 and netted $50,000. By being resourceful and creative, pay as you go can be an effective strategy for financing a business.

Pay as You Go Promoting for Your Business Start-Up
If you need to start from scratch, Pay as You Go Promoting is the way to go.

My goal was to build my business on a pay as I go basis. The challenge was to find ways to do promotion and marketing on a very low budget. This starts out slowly and builds. It develops your resourcefulness and creativity.

The first thing I did was to take advantage of free communication through personal networking and social network sites on the internet, getting listed on the Internet.

Next I decided to use direct mail marketing. I didn't have a list of email contacts who had opted in to receive my messages, so instead of email, I send out actual marketing letters instead. Now with direct mail there are firms that sell lists and or do your entire mailing for you at a cost of thousands of dollars. But I decided on a do it myself approach on a much smaller scale.

Jeffrey Dobkin's books, *How to Market A Product for Under $500*, and *Uncommon Marketing Techniques* are great resources for direct mail marketing. Although these are both pretty much pre-Internet marketing, and parts of them are less relevant to today's reality, I highly recommend both of these books as classics in the field of direct marketing. In the beginning I had no money for brochures. Jeff shows how to write your own letter and send to your prospects without a brochure, which can easily be adapted to email.

I started a mailing list in a file on my pc, but I usually address my letters by hand. Also, if you like commemorative stamps add a nice touch. People are more likely to open this type of mail that looks interesting, than ones with mailing labels, or email for that matter.

The key to pay as you go marketing is consistency. Instead of simply sending one letter to your prospects, you write a series of letters for a campaign. Instead of putting out some ads, and then forgetting about it, you have to put more ads out with some regularity. In this way you will start to build momentum in your business. As you make sales, you can then use the money to invest in more promotions.

26 SECRETS OF EFFECTIVE PROSPECTING

Prospecting is as necessary to business as ever, and essential to making sales. Prospecting is not selling. Rather it is a process of contacting, sorting and identifying potential customers, and to connect with those who are interested in what you have to offer. Thus prospecting is an initial step in the sales process.

Yet aspiring entrepreneurs and marketers tend to avoid prospecting like the plague.

There are a number of myths about prospecting, such as it takes too much time, or it does not work. Instead, so-called "Attraction Marketing" is often touted as a method of branding or marketing oneself so as to generate eager customers who will show up ready to buy from you.

There are a number of systems currently being offered that claim to streamline, automate or package this process for you, so that you will not have to stumble and struggle with prospecting. Many of the gurus who claim expert status are not actually engaged in marketing any product or opportunity other than their own system or affiliate products. They make their fortunes with bait and switch tactics of exploiting the inexperienced entrepreneur's fears of failure and rejection.

But really, there is no substitute for having actual conversations with people to find out what they want and need, and whether what you have to offer is the right fit for them.

Granted, prospecting can be awkward or embarrassing in the beginning, but as with any thing else, there are skills that can be learned, improved upon and mastered with practice.

When I started my network marketing business, my company training, like most others, was mainly focused on making a list of my warm market or buying leads. I found that once I had exhausted my warm market, I became anxious about where to find more prospects. I did not find purchasing leads productive either, so I kept searching for more ways to find new customers, and eventually found more resources for learning new prospecting methods.

Doing so, I have come to appreciate that these are skills that anyone can learn who wants to make an effort. And as you do so, prospecting just gets easier and easier.

27 MONITORING COSTS AND RETURNS

How much is too much to invest in your business?

Marketing your business effectively will be an ongoing expense. There is no way to get exposure and gain customers without spending money on a regular basis. But simply throwing money into advertising is not cost effective and may not bring the desired results.

It is important to be creative and resourceful to make the best use of your funds. You can augment your budget by using some free resources such as social media online, but you most likely will still need to spend money for paid advertisements as well.

It is best to establish a budget based on your business plan and stay within your budget. To determine the effectiveness or your marketing investment, you will need to look at your return on investment. What profit is derived from the money that you spend?

Advertising that is aimed at anyone and everyone is not cost effective for the money spent.

A more effective marketing strategy is to decide on what demographic groups would be most interested in what you are offering, and focus your efforts on reaching them. For example, you might have a service or product of interest to golfers, or gardeners, or pet owners.

You would then develop specific advertisements to be aimed at your target customers, and place the ads in specific media of interest to your niche group. Keep track of your results to check on which ads produced the best return on your investment. For example, you might use some simple coupon codes on different offers, or ask the customer where they heard about your business.

Because marketing and advertising are ongoing expenses, it is important to monitor your expenses. Use a mix of different types of marketing channels, both online and offline. Keep records of your customers' contact information so that you can stay in contact them and let them know about additional offers.

28 MEASURING BUSINESS RESUTLTS AT YEAR'S END

"A definition of insanity is to keep doing the same thing and getting the same results."-- Albert Einstein

As the last week of the year rolls around, it's important to review and reflect on what I have accomplished as I look ahead to the next year and make plans. It's always helpful to just hit the pause button and assess how things are going. This is an ongoing process, which I like to do as I go along, but as the year turns over a wider picture emerges.

Conditions are constantly changing, even week to week and month to month. I have learned that one of the best ways to measure what's effective is by keeping track of numbers, to determine my Return on Investment. That way I can break down how much I am investing in time and money, and how much profit results from that investment of activity and money.

I confess that it took me a long time to start doing this, as I've never been good at quantifiable data keeping. So in the past anything having to do with numbers has been something I procrastinated on and put off as long as possible. Therefore, my evaluations suffered from vagueness of both time and numbers.

I have become increasingly aware of time management. I used to assume that I was okay with my time management. I followed a system of setting priorities, and as long as I accomplished my main priorities, I felt that was good enough.

But when I began to actually study time management, I realized that my time management system was rather vague. This vagueness left a lot of holes. I was wasting time as it slipped through holes much like water pouring through the holes in a strainer.

By keeping track of numbers, one can then evaluate how effective a given strategy is by tracking the numbers and reviewing them over time. For example, if X number of dollars and Y number of hours are spent on it, and what results were achieved. That would be the ROI for the investment made.

Breaking it down in the short term provides you with a snapshot, but over the long term, a larger picture will emerge. As I analyzed various activities in my business more by the numbers, I saw which ones were more or less effective, and I was able to let go of those that were not achieving results.

After using the ROI process, I made the following changes: deleted my Facebook business page, stopped going to meetings of a local networking group, and stopped sending out email newsletters

Time is our most precious resource, as it can never be replaced. The more I am mindful of time, and keeping track of how I spend my time, I see more ways that I can use my time effectively, and eliminate those things that are not a a productive use of my time.

As you become more efficient at managing my time, you have more free time available to spend on doing the things that are most important to you.

29 TYPES OF BUSINESS STRUCTURES

There are various ways to establish a business structure, depending on the nature of the enterprise. The most common types include sole proprietorship, partnership, Limited Liability Company (LLC), non-profit, and franchising.

If you plan to start a business out of your home, you can organize as a sole proprietor and start with a much smaller investment. Some service businesses are limited to a locality, while others may be marketed via the Internet to a wider range of customers.

A sole proprietorship, also known as the sole trader or simply a proprietorship, is a type of business that is owned and run by one natural person and in which there is no legal distinction between the owner and the business. The owner is in direct control of all elements and is legally accountable for the finances of such business and this may include debts, loans, loss etc.

The owner receives all profits (subject to taxation specific to the business) and has unlimited responsibility for all losses and debts. Every asset of the business is owned by the proprietor and all debts of the business are the proprietor's. It is a "sole" proprietorship in contrast with business partnerships (which have at least 2 owners).

A sole proprietor may use a trade name or business name other than his, her or its legal name. They will have to legally trademark their business name, the process being different depending upon country of residence.

A partnership is an arrangement in which two or more persons, known as partners, agree to cooperate to advance their mutual interests in a business.

A limited liability company (LLC) is the United States-specific form of a private limited company. It is a business structure that combines the pass-through taxation of a partnership or sole proprietorship with the limited liability of a corporation. An LLC is not a corporation; it is a legal form of a company that provides limited liability to its owners in many jurisdictions. LLCs do not need to be organized for profit. In certain U.S. states (for example, Texas), businesses that provide professional services requiring a state professional license, such as legal or medical services, may not be allowed to form an LLC but may be required to form a very similar entity called a Professional Limited

Franchising is the practice of the right to use a firms successful business brand and model for a prescribed period of time. The word "franchise" is of Anglo-French derivation—from franc, meaning free—and is used both as a noun and as a (transitive) verb. For the franchiser, the franchise is an alternative to building "chain stores" to distribute goods that avoids the investments and liability of a chain.
Buying into a franchise requires substantially more money to invest, as well as ongoing fees each year. An advantage of a franchise is that much of the advertising and marketing are provided by the company. To operate a franchise, you may need to hire employees.

The franchisor's success depends on the success of the franchisees. The franchisee is said to have a greater incentive than a direct employee because he or she has a direct stake in the business. Essentially, and in terms of distribution, the franchisor is a supplier who allows an operator, or a franchisee, to use the supplier's trademark and distribute the supplier's goods. In return, the operator pays the supplier a fee.

Thirty three countries—including the United States and Australia—have laws that explicitly regulate franchising, with the majority of all other countries having laws which have a direct or indirect impact on franchising.

A Nonprofit organization (NPO, also known as a non-business entity) is an organization that uses its surplus revenues to further achieve its purpose or mission, rather than distributing its surplus income to the organization's directors (or equivalents) as profit or dividends. This is known as the distribution constraint.

The decision to adopt a nonprofit legal structure is one which often has taxation implications too, particularly where the nonprofit seeks income tax exemption, charitable status and so on.

BIBLIOGRAPHY

As A Man Thinketh, James Allen
Mary Kay, Mary Kay Ash
How I Raised Myself From Failure to Success in Selling, Frank Bettger
Endless Referrals Network Your Everyday Contacts Into Sales, Bob Burg
The Power of Focus, Jack Canfield, Mark Victor Hansen, Les Hewitt
The Success Principals, Jack Canfield
How to Win Friends and Influence People, Dale Carnegie
The Seven Habits of Highly Effective People, Stephen Covey
How to Market a Product for Under $500, Jeffrey Dobkin
Uncommon Marketing Techniques, Jeffrey Dobkin
The 4-Hour Work Week, Timothy Ferriss
Creative Visualization Using the Power of Your Imagination to Create What You Want in Life, Shakti Gawain
Outliers, Malcolm Gladwell
The Tipping Point, Malcolm Gladwell
Purple Cow, Seth Godin
Think and Grow Rich, Napoleon Hill
How to Master the Art of Selling, Tom Hopkins
No BS Sales Success in the New Economy, Dan S. Kennedy
Rich Dad, Poor Dad, Robert Kiyosaki
Guerrilla Marketing, Jay Conrad Levinson
Develop the Leader Within You, John Maxwell
Pink Slip Proof-- How to Control All Future Paychecks, Paul J. Meyer
Anything You Want, Derek Sivers
The Psychology of Selling, Brian Tracy
Crush It, Gary Vaynerchuck
The Thank You Economy, Gary Vaynerchuck
The Art of Closing the Sale, Zig Ziglar
Ziglar on Selling, Zig Ziglar

About Deborah Gorman

Deborah is a life coach, business consultant and writer. She has been a journalist, whose work has appeared in numerous publications. She has also been a pastor, teacher and entrepreneur.
Deborah is originally from the Midwestern US, and now makes her home in North Carolina.
She enjoys hiking, gardening, travel and exploring new places.

Deborah has published two previous books:

Free and Clear: Master Your Money and Escape the Debt Trap
Essentials of Starting Your Business

www.ingramcontent.com/pod-product-compliance
Lightning Source LLC
Chambersburg PA
CBHW020928180526
45163CB00007B/2927